Changing Materials
Heating

Chris Oxlade

Heinemann Library
Chicago, Illinois

www.heinemannraintree.com
Visit our website to find out more information about Heinemann-Raintree books.

To order:
☎ Phone 888-454-2279
🖥 Visit www.heinemannraintree.com to browse our catalog and order online.

© 2009 Heinemann Library
an imprint of Capstone Global Library, LLC
Chicago, Illinois

Customer Service: 888-454-2279

Visit our website at www.heinemannraintree.com

Edited by Charlotte Guillain and Rebecca Rissman
Designed by Ryan Frieson and Betsy Wernert
Original illustrations © Capstone Global Library Ltd.
Illustrated by Randy Schirz (p. 8)
Illustrated by Hart McLeod (pp. 11)
Photo research by Elizabeth Alexander and Virginia Stroud-Lewis
Printed and bound by South China Printing Company Ltd.

13 12 11 10 09
10 9 8 7 6 5 4 3 2 1

Library of Congress Cataloging-in-Publication Data
Oxlade, Chris.
  Heating / Chris Oxlade.
    p. cm. -- (Changing materials)
  Includes bibliographical references and index.
  ISBN 978-1-4329-3272-5 (hc) -- ISBN 978-1-4329-3277-0
(pb) 1. Heat--Juvenile literature. 2. Materials--Thermal
properties--Juvenile literature. 3. Change of state (Physics)--
Juvenile literature. I. Title.
  QC256.O95 2009
  530.4'74--dc22
                                                2008054588

Acknowledgments

The author and publishers are grateful to the following for permission to reproduce copyright material: : Alamy **pp. 6** (© Ilya Shadrin), **15** (© Timothy Herzel), **17** (© Adrian Sherratt/Alamy), **21** (Peter Bowater), **23** (© Richard Church), **24** (© superclic), **26** (© foodfolio); © Capstone Global Library **pp. 4, 5** (MM Studios); © Capstone Publishers **pp. 7, 28, 29** (Karon Dubke); Corbis **pp. 13** (© Jason Hosking/zefa), **27** (© Charles O'Rear); iStockphoto **p. 22** (© Leah-Anne Thompson); Photolibrary **p. 10** (Frank Wieder Photography/ Fresh Food Images); Science Photo Library **pp. 9** (Martyn F. Chillmaid), **18** (Martin Dohrn); Shutterstock **pp. 12** (© ulga), **14** (© AXL), **16** (© Luis Francisco Cordero), **19** (© CAN BALCIOGLU), **20** (© Stephen Orsillo), **25** (© Trutta55).

Cover photograph of a steaming kettle reproduced with permission of iStockphoto/© Rick Lord.

Every effort has been made to contact copyright holders of material reproduced in this book. Any omissions will be rectified in subsequent printings if notice is given to the publisher.

All the Internet addresses (URLs) given in this book were valid at the time of going to press. However, due to the dynamic nature of the Internet, some addresses may have changed, or sites may have changed or ceased to exist since publication. While the author and Publishers regret any inconvenience this may cause readers, no responsibility for any such changes can be accepted by either the author or the Publishers.

Contents

Words appearing in the text in bold, **like this**, are explained in the glossary.

About Materials

How many different types of materials can you think of? Do you see any wood, plastic, or metal in this photo? These are all materials we use to make things.

Can you name the different materials in this photograph?

How many of these things are made from materials made by humans?

Some materials are **natural** materials. We get them from the world around us. Soil, cotton, and rubber are natural materials. Humans make other materials, such as glass and metals.

Changing Materials

When water cools down, it turns into ice.

Materials can change shape. Sometimes we can change the **properties** of a material. The properties of a material include how it looks and feels.

Materials often change when we heat them up. Heating a material makes it warmer, or hotter.

This ice is **melting** because the child's hands are warming it.

Different Materials

Most materials we see are **solid** materials. But some are **liquids**, like water. And some are **gases**, like the air around us.

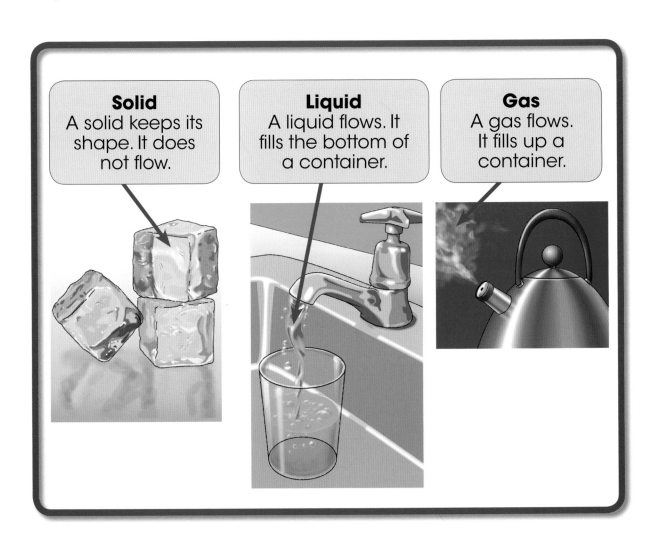

Solid
A solid keeps its shape. It does not flow.

Liquid
A liquid flows. It fills the bottom of a container.

Gas
A gas flows. It fills up a container.

When a solid material heats up, it can turn into a liquid. When a liquid heats up, it can turn into a gas.

When liquid water is heated, it turns into bubbles of gas.

Hot and Cold

Some things in the world around us are hot and some are cold. We can tell if things are warm or cool by touching them. But hot things, such as ovens and irons, can burn you, so it is important to be careful.

This food is hot.
This drink is cold.

Temperature tells us how cold or how hot something is. The temperature of a cold thing is lower than the temperature of a hot thing. Temperature is measured in degrees Fahrenheit (°F) or degrees Celsius (°C).

We measure temperature with a **thermometer**.

°C
100
90
80
70
60
50
40
30
20
10
0

°F
212
190
170
150
130
110
90
70
50
32

Heating Up

Heat is going into this pot, making it hotter.

To heat up a material, we must add heat to it. The heat goes into the material and makes its **temperature** go up.

There are many ways to heat things up. Holding something near a fire makes it warmer. Putting something in an oven or in sunlight also heats it up.

The meat on a grill cooks because it is heated by the fire below it.

Melting

When we warm up some **solid** materials, they turn into **liquids**. Ice is a solid. When it warms up, it turns into water, which is a liquid.

Warm weather heats ice. The ice turns into water.

Solid wax melts when it is heated by a candle's flame.

When a solid turns into a liquid, it changes. This change is called **melting**.

Melting Points

This ice is turning into water at 32°F (0°C).

A material always **melts** at the same **temperature**. For example, ice always melts at 32°F (0°C). This is called the **melting point** of ice.

Some materials do not melt until they are at a much higher temperature than 32°F (0°C). For example, pans are made of metal because metal has a very high melting point. The pans will not melt on the stove or in the oven.

This metal is so hot that it is glowing red. It has started to melt and is soft enough to bend.

Boiling

When we warm up some **liquids**, they change into **gases**. For example, water changes into a gas when you heat it up in a pot. The gas is called steam or **water vapor**.

You can see bubbles of gas in the water as it boils.

The gas that comes from a tea pot's spout is steam, or water vapor.

When a liquid turns into a gas, the material changes. This change is called **boiling**.

Boiling Points

A **liquid** always **boils** at the same **temperature**. For example, water always boils at 212°F (100°C). This is called the **boiling point** of water.

Water always turns into steam, or **water vapor**, at 212°F (100°C).

Other liquids have to be much hotter before they boil. A metal must be very hot before it will boil.

This metal is very hot. It has turned into liquid metal but it is still not hot enough to boil.

Investigating Heating Up

When you have been outside on a cold winter day, your hands may feel freezing. How many ways can you think of to warm them up again?

Breathing on your hands warms them up because your breath is warm.

Rubbing your hands together is a way to warm them up. This works because of **friction** between your hands. Rubbing any materials together makes friction and warms them up.

Friction makes heat when you rub your hands.

Sources of Heat

To make something hotter, we have to add heat to it. Cooking on a stove heats something up.

Heat from a stove makes the water **boil**.

Heat in the Sun's rays makes the sand warm.

The Sun also heats things up. During the day, heat from the sun warms materials. For example, on a hot day at the beach, the sand feels hot under your feet because the Sun has heated it.

Changing Properties

Heating up a material can change the material's **properties**. Often they cannot be changed back. For example, cake batter changes when you put it into a hot oven.

Runny cake batter changes into a **solid**, spongy cake when it is heated.

When a material is burned, we can never get it back. When you put wood on a bonfire, the wood burns and turns to ash. The wood is gone forever.

Wood is changing into ash on top of this fire.

Investigating Escaping Gas

This simple experiment will show you that **gases** grow to fill up more space when they are heated.

You will need:

✳ a large, empty, plastic drink bottle

✳ a small coin that will cover the bottle's neck

Activity

1) Dip a small coin in water and put it over the bottle's neck.
2) Very gently put your hands around the bottle. Just touch the bottle, without squeezing it.

What happens

Heat from your hands warms the air in the bottle. The air spreads out and pushes up against the coin, making it jump.

2

Glossary

boiling when a material changes from liquid to gas

boiling point temperature at which a material always boils

friction force that tries to stop two surfaces from sliding against each other

gas material that flows and fills a space. Air is a gas.

liquid material that flows and fills the bottom of a container. Water is a liquid.

melting when a material changes from solid to liquid

melting point temperature at which a material always melts

natural something that is not made by people. It comes from animals, plants, or the rocks of the Earth.

property thing that tells us what a material is like, such as how it feels and looks

solid material that stays in shape and does not flow. Wood is a solid.

temperature measure of how hot or cold something is

thermometer tool for measuring how hot or cold something is

water vapor gas form of water, made when water boils

Find Out More

Books

Llewellyn, Claire. *Exploring Materials.* Mankato, Minn.:
Sea to Sea, 2009.

Manolis, Kay. *Temperature.* Minneapolis:
Bellwether, 2008.

Oxlade, Chris. *Using Materials* series (*Coal, Cotton, Glass,
Metal, Oil, Paper, Plastic, Rock, Rubber, Silk, Soil, Water,
Wood, Wool*). Chicago: Heinemann Library, 2004–2005.

Stille, Darlene R. *Heating Up and Cooling Down.*
Minneapolis: Picture Window, 2004.

Websites

www.crickweb.co.uk/assets/resources/flash.
php?&file=materials

www.crickweb.co.uk/assets/resources/flash.
php?&file=materials2d
Visit these web pages for interactive science activities.

Index